# AUTHOR'S NOTE:

ALS, or amyotrophic lateral sclerosis, is a progressive neurodegenerative disease that currently has no cure. ALS is a disease that typically involves a gradual onset, with initial symptoms that can be quite varied in different people. One person may struggle with lifting a coffee cup or grasping a pen, while others may begin slurring or losing their speech - ALS affects everyone differently. Regardless, ALS is a disease that always takes - takes someone's ability to help themselves, takes someone's ability to express themselves, and ultimately takes someone from the ones who love them most.

Mom was taken from us by this disease too soon. She was a nurse of over 30 years, always taking care of others, to end up being taken care of herself. Though we ultimately lost Mom to ALS, we gained a purpose to bring awareness and support to others who may have or had the same experience with their loved one. Whether it's Mom, Dad, Grandma, Grandpa, or another loved one affected by this disease that always takes, always remember - but they still can love.

For more ALS information and resources, visit als.org. A large portion of the proceeds from this book will benefit the ALS Association of Georgia Chapter's 'Walk to Defeat ALS' in honor of Mom, Marina Pascarelli.

Dedicated to the bravest woman I know.

Grandma has ALS, and her messengers in her brain may not be able to talk to her muscles anymore, but she still can love.

Grandma may not be able
to pick me up anymore,
but she still can love.

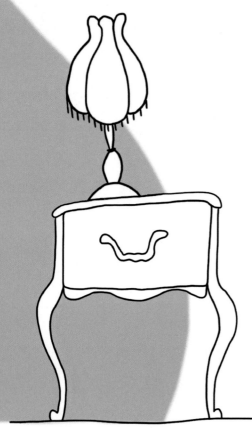

Grandma may not be able
to walk with me anymore,
but she still can love.

Grandma may not be able to
drive me around in her car
anymore, but she still can love.

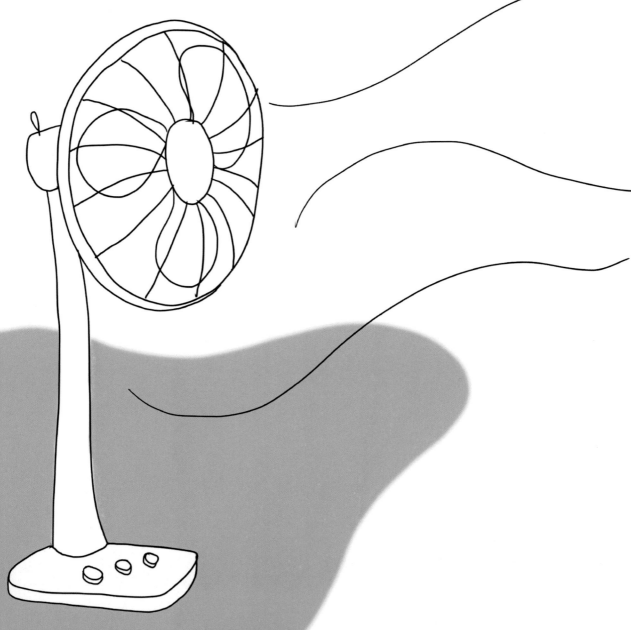

Grandma may not be able to
cook dinner for me anymore,
but she still can love.

Grandma may not be able to
dance on her feet anymore,
but she still can love.

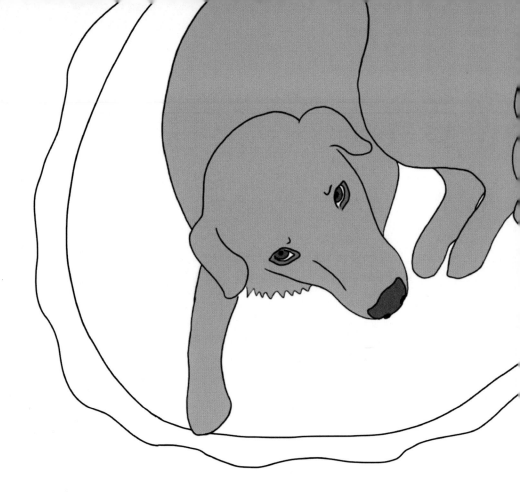

Grandma may not be able to
turn the page of a book
anymore, but she still can love.

Grandma may not be able to feed herself anymore, but she still can love.

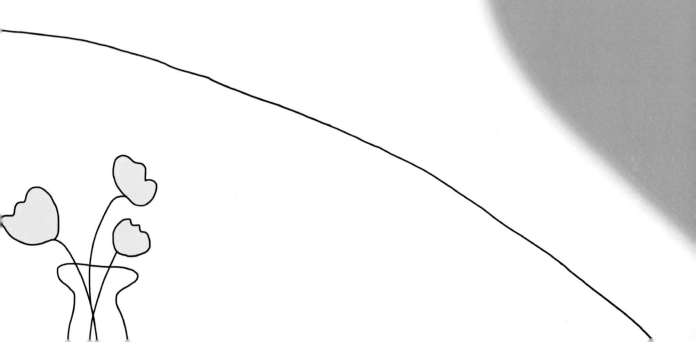

Grandma may not be able to breathe on her own without the help of her "space mask" anymore, but she still can love.

Grandma may not be able to use her voice to talk to me anymore, but she still can love.

Grandma may not be able to be here on this Earth anymore, but she still can love.

# HOME

I can jump
I can eat
I can sing
I can walk

I can move
I can dance
I can breathe
I can talk

I am home
I am healed
I am free
I am whole

I now have
So much more
Than ALS stole

The race has been finished
My journey is done
Please don't say, "He lost his battle"
For indeed, I HAVE WON

**Steve Martin**
ALS hero & advocate, 3.21.2021

Made in the USA
Las Vegas, NV
21 November 2021